MURPHY'S
LAWS
OF GOLF

MURPHY'S LAWS
OF GOLF

HENRY BEARD

ILLUSTRATED BY PHIL SCHEUER

Sterling Publishing Co., Inc.
New York

A JOHN BOSWELL ASSOCIATES BOOK

Library of Congress
Cataloging-in-Publication Data Available

2   4   6   8   10   9   7   5   3   1

Published by Sterling Publishing Co., Inc.
387 Park Avenue South, New York, NY 10016
© 2007 by Sterling Publishing Co., Inc.

Distributed in Canada by Sterling Publishing
c/o Canadian Manda Group, 165 Dufferin Street
Toronto, Ontario, Canada M6K 3H6
Distributed in the United Kingdom by GMC Distribution Services
Castle Place, 166 High Street, Lewes, East Sussex, England BN7 1XU
Distributed in Australia by Capricorn Link (Australia) Pty. Ltd.
P.O. Box 704, Windsor, NSW 2756, Australia

Printed in China

Sterling ISBN-13: 978-1-4027-4775-5
ISBN-10: 1-4027-4775-6

For information about custom editions, special
sales, premium and corporate purchases, please contact
Sterling Special Sales Department at 800-805-5489
or specialsales@sterlingpub.com.

design Nan Jernigan

INTRODUCTION

BACK IN THE early days of golf, when the first rules were written ("Play it as it lies"; "Kick it if no one is looking") and the basics of etiquette were formulated ("Use the clubs to hit the ball, not the other players"; "Don't pee in the hole"), there simultaneously appeared, pretty much out of nowhere, a series of shrewd and rueful observations about the game that were nearly always attributed to a mysterious individual named Murphy.

As time passed, these canny precepts ("If something can go wrong, it will, and at the worst possible time") and savvy admonitions ("If it ain't broke, don't fix it") found their way into the worlds of business, the military, government, science, and economics. But the roots of the by now legendary Murphy's Laws clearly lie in golf, a sport that seems to have been tailor made to expose the fundamental malevolence of the cosmos.

For where else but on a golf course could anyone so swiftly conclude that nature is not simply indifferent but actually hostile, and that, far from being blind, fate has superb eyesight and a mean streak a mile wide?

After all, long before the paradoxical principles of quantum mechanics were discovered, golfers had already had ample opportunity to experience the sheer perversity of the universe firsthand: they watched in baffled disbelief as their balls repeatedly disappeared into other dimensions, their shots veered off at impossible angles, space curved sharply to the right, time ran backwards in the presence of women, gravity was regularly defied, and the laws of motion were constantly contravened.

Whether Murphy was an actual historical character and the two hundred and fifty axioms, maxims, laws, and dictates that bear his name truly are the work of some solitary Einstein of the links is almost beside the point. Whatever their source, these astonishing nuggets of golfing wisdom represent one of the greatest contributions to the understanding of the game ever made and, taken together, provide a foolproof guide to its manifold frustrations.

Well, almost foolproof. This book, like everything connected to golf (and just about anything else) is subject to the unforgiving effects of Murphy's great theory, and so, if there are any misprints, or upside-down pages, or any other laughable boo-boos, please accept in advance the auther's sinecrest appologies.

Murphy's
FIRST PRINCIPLES

The game of golf is 90% mental and 10% mental

Anything that can go right
will go way, way right

Anything that can go wrong will
wait to go wrong until after you
leave the practice tee

All current problems can be traced to previous solutions

No matter how badly you're playing, you can always play worse

Whatever you think you're doing wrong is the one thing you're doing right

If it ain't broke, don't fiddle with your grip

Anything works for three holes

What worked yesterday won't work today

It won't work tomorrow, either

There are no little problems

There are no minor adjustments

There are no tiny pieces of advice

The reason you do so well on
the range is because it's really not all
that hard to hit the horizon in regulation

The only thing of actual value that you can
take from the range to the first tee is
a pocketful of range balls

The only time you play absolutely
flawless golf is when you are doing
everything in your power to lose to
the boss

Everyone would like to get much better
at golf, but they'll settle for you playing
a whole lot worse

If you address the ball more for more than twenty seconds, it's not a waggle — it's a seizure

It's often necessary to hit a second drive to really appreciate the first one

Hit the do-over first

To hit a truly awful shot in golf, mere incompetence is not enough—you really need an audience

If you can keep your head when the wheels come off, you need a new head

Tennis would be as difficult as golf
if you only got one serve, six-love was par,
you had to wait ten minutes between points,
you often lost a dozen balls in a single set,
and every now and then you needed to hit a
backhand out of a tree

The reason so many golfers take up fly-fishing is that the motion of casting with the rod is easily mastered by anyone who ever threw a club

The reason golf is so popular is that it gives people cooped up in the office all week a chance to lie and cheat outdoors

The stages of a golfer's game are: Sudden Collapse, Radical Change, Complete Frustration, Slow Improvement, Brief Mastery, and Sudden Collapse

All change is for the worse, except for underwear

Murphy's
DOCTRINE OF THE LINKS

You can always nail the drive
on a hole with no carry

Hazards attract

Fairways repel

Trees never stop crooked shots

The shortest distance between any two points on a golf hole is a straight line that passes directly through the center of a very large tree

The worse your drive is stymied, the more perfectly it would have played on the previous hole

Nothing straightens out a slice
faster than a sharp dogleg to the right

When hitting a ball out of the woods,
remember that trees are mostly air, just
like screen doors and practice nets

Out of Bounds is always on the right

Two-thirds of the holes are uphill

The wind is in your face on 15 of the holes

The tees are always back

The rough will be mown tomorrow

The rake is in the other bunker

Electric carts never die at the turn

It never starts raining in the middle of the 18th hole

No one ever got a blister walking to the first tee

The practice putting green is much faster or a lot slower than the rest of the greens on the course

On courses where the yardage is on the sprinkler heads, the nearest one will be 40 yards away, it will be blank, and it will turn on as you're looking at it

There's no ground that couldn't
use a little repair

It's always winter somewhere

Remember, there are no referees in golf—
it's up to you and you alone to decide if
you're entitled to a free kick

The pro shop has the kind of glove
you like, but not your size

All the hats are yellow

The only cheap balls are Top Flite X-outs

A bag of tees costs four bucks

If you stop for lunch between nines, you will overhear a conversation featuring the words "choke" and "shank"

If you stop for a beer at the end of the round, you will hear someone bitching about shooting a 78

The fancier the course, the greater the risk of food poisoning

The people who buy houses on golf courses always seem surprised to discover that a game in which balls are hit with considerable force is being played practically in their backyards

The people on the greenkeeping staff always look like they took the job because a golf course is such a perfect place to dispose of all the bodies

If you had to get up at five in the
morning, got paid peanuts for working
like a dog outdoors the whole day in
all kinds of weather, and then took a
lot of crap from a bunch of jerks, where
would you put the pins?

Murphy's
AXIOMS OF BALL AERODYNAMICS

A ball will always travel farthest when
hit in the wrong direction

A ball will never lip out of a pot bunker
or burn the edge of a pond

You can draw the ball, you can fade the
ball, but no one can straight the ball

A ball will always come to rest halfway
down a slope unless there is sand or water
at the bottom

A ball at rest on a steep slope will tend
to remain at rest until the moment it is
addressed

The harder you try to keep your ball from landing in a particular place, the more certain it is to go there

A ball will always seek the lowest point in which to lie so long as that point is not a perfectly round hole 4 1/2 inches in diameter and 4 inches deep

If there is a ball in the fringe and a ball in the bunker, your ball is in the bunker

If both balls are in the bunker, yours is in the footprint

A ball that looked stiff to the pin from
back in the fairway will be ten feet from
the hole when you get to the green

The only time you can put the ball
exactly where you want it is when
you stick it in the ballwasher

A ball hit into the rough will always disappear between two identical shrubs

A ball you can see in the rough from 50 yards away is not yours

If you can't find your ball in the rough, but you do find another ball that you could easily play, it will be orange, yellow, or pink

The fewer balls you have, the more balls you lose; the more balls you have, the more balls you lose

A ball you searched for for five minutes will be found in five seconds by a player in the first group behind you

Before you drop a ball, always decide whether you're going for accuracy or distance

The only sure way to find a drive sliced deep into the woods is to hit a provisional ball right down the middle of the fairway

The only sure way to hit a perfectly straight 250-yard drive is to decide not to go for it on a dogleg hole

The only sure way to get a hole-in-one is to be playing terrible golf all by yourself on a course you sneaked onto without paying on a day when you called in sick

Murphy's
MAXIMS OF COURSE MANAGEMENT

The key to target golf is choosing a really, really big target

It's a simple matter to keep your ball in the fairway if you're not too choosy about which fairway

You can hit a 2-acre fairway 10% of the time, and a 2-inch branch 90% of the time

You can put your ball in even the smallest fairway bunker if you pick it as an aiming point

If you have to hit a drive over a
ravine, you need to make up your
mind whether you're going to hit
a good shot short with a shit ball,
or a shit shot short with a good ball

When your tee shot has to carry over
a water hazard, you can either hit one
more club or two more balls

No matter how short the par-3,
never line up the logo when you tee
up your ball or plumb-bob the hole
with your wedge

Never wash your ball on the tee of
a water hole

If you're afraid a full shot might reach the green 200 yards away while the foursome in front of you is putting out, you have two options: You can go ahead and hit and rip the shot of your life onto the green on the fly, or you can wait until the green is clear and cold-top a ball halfway there

There are two kinds of bounces: unfair bounces, and bounces just the way you meant to play it

Never claim that you intended to skip the ball across the water or hop it along the cart path or stop it against a rake handle

Aiming for the dead center of a bridge that crosses a creek in the middle of the fairway is seldom the percentage shot

Everyone sees a whiff, but no one is ever looking when you hit a career shot

Never curse a god-awful shot until it has had a chance to get lucky

Always leave yourself a full shank

The odds against parring another hole double after every hole you par

The reason it's so hard to par the course is half the shots are woods, half the shots are irons, and the third half is putts

The most difficult lie in golf is a
ball sitting up in a perfect lie in the
dead center of the fairway 150 yards
from the pin

If you absolutely, positively have to par
a hole, leave a birdie putt one inch short

To blow up on the back nine you
don't need to have played a terrific
front nine, but it certainly doesn't hurt

The reason it's called "golf" is that all the
really good four-letter words were already
taken

If you can only play a few holes, you'll be two under par when you have to leave

It takes 17 holes to really get warmed up

Murphy's
PRECEPTS OF CLUB SELECTION

Nothing cools off a putter quicker than a hot driver

It's the right club, but you decide it's
the wrong club

It's the right club, but you think it
might be too little club so you try to
kill it, or it might be too much club,
so you quit on the shot

It's the wrong club

A ten-foot putt counts just the same as
a ten-foot drive

You can hit the ball 30 yards with any club
in the bag

You really need only four clubs to hit every
bad shot in golf

Your straightest iron shot of the day will be exactly one club short

If you want to hit a 7-iron as far as John Daly does, simply play to lay up just short of a water hazard

You can't hit decent tee shots with a 3-wood unless you carry a driver you never use

Even if it's a 5-iron, the lowest numbered iron in your bag will always be impossible to hit

When you're between clubs, it's always the other club, unless it's the other other club

When someone asks what club you hit, always subtract one or add two

When in doubt, just ask yourself, What would Tiger hit?, and use six more clubs

If you have to keep the cart on the cart path, unless you take every single one of your clubs over to your ball, you won't have the right club

It always takes at least five holes to notice that a club is missing

Everyone turns in a 2-iron, but you can kiss that wedge good-bye

The best way to cause the reappearance of a club lost on the course is to order a replacement

Funny-looking putters have short lifespans

The reason those fancy wedges are so expensive is they come with a free case of the shanks

The week after you break down and buy
one of those super-duper new drivers,
they'll knock a hundred bucks off the price
and release a brand new model with a
better shaft and a bigger head

You haven't really hit bottom until you
need to get your ball retriever regripped

The best thing about a 60-degree wedge
is it's a great club for getting
the ball out of the lies you're going to
end up in if you're dumb enough to use
a 60-degree wedge

The best thing about hybrids is that
no one can tell that your 150-yard club
used to be a wood, not an iron

Never ask the pro if you need a new set of clubs

Never buy a putter until you've had a chance to throw it

Never hit trick shots with demo clubs

Murphy's
LAWS OF GOLF PHYSICS

A stroke does not count unless it has been observed by another golfer

Bets lengthen putts and shorten drives

Confidence evaporates in the presence
of water

In the heat of a match, balls tend to rise
to the surface of the rough

99.99% of the universe is empty space, but that last .01% will stop a golf ball dead

If the moon had a more evenly dimpled surface and a hard rubber core, a couple of Out of Bounds stakes could pull it out of its orbit

There are four forces affecting the motion of a golf ball:

1. *Gravity*, which causes the ball to drop suddenly into hazards
2. *Electromagnetism*, which makes the ball curve sharply towards whichever of the earth's poles is closest to the Out of Bounds stakes
3. *The Weak Force*, which makes the ball dribble to the ladies' tee
4. *The Strong Force*, which propels the ball directly towards a foursome of personal injury lawyers in the adjacent fairway

*E*very time a golfer makes a birdie, he must subsequently make two triple bogeys to restore the equilibrium of the universe

It takes a whole lot of pressure to make a penalty stroke adhere to a scorecard

Matter can be neither created nor destroyed, but it can be bent double, broken in half, stomped on, and hurled a considerable distance

The number of tees in the ball pocket
of your bag is always less than 3 or more
than 600

Removing raingear from the pocket of
a golf bag instantly doubles its weight
and triples its volume

Even if a ball retriever extends to 40 feet,
it will always be one foot too short to reach
the ball

A golf vacation is a trip taken by two or
more players to a place where no one can
remember when it rained so much

The first golf bag down the chute of the
airport luggage carousel belongs to a player
waiting for it on another continent

If you brought it, you won't need it;
if you need it, you didn't bring it

Strokes always accumulate faster than they can be forgotten

Since bad shots come in groups of three, a fourth bad shot is actually the first of the next group of three

One birdie is a hot streak

Shooting your age is not a realistic goal—focus on shooting your weight

It's easier to shrink your shoe size than to lower your handicap

If you really want to get better at golf, go back and take it up at a much earlier age

Murphy's
SWING THEORIES

Anyone can groove a good, solid, repeatable practice swing

It doesn't count as a swing thought if it's phrased as a prayer

The more memorable the swing thought, the more useless the information it conveys

Never try to keep more than thirty separate thoughts in your mind during your swing

When you hit a horrible shot because you looked up, you will always look down again just at the moment when you ought to start watching the ball if you ever want to see it again

When the wind is in your face, you swing too hard to try to compensate for it; when the wind is at your back, you swing too hard to try to take advantage of it

When you play in a mixed foursome, there will always be at least one hole where you have to hit your second shot before the ladies tee off

It's a waste of time to videotape your swing—what you need is duct tape

The only thing you can learn from your mistakes is to stop paying the pro a hundred and fifty bucks to point them out to you

You're never going to get anywhere in golf until you convert that nasty slice into a wicked hook

There is no movement in the golf swing so difficult that it cannot be made even more difficult by careful study and diligent practice

The most likely effect of a lesson is
to instantly eliminate the one key flaw
in your grip or stance that allowed you
to somehow compensate for all the other
faults in your swing

Any swing drill or shotmaking tip that
you just couldn't get the hang of during
a one-hour lesson will be immediately
mastered by the first player you describe
it to

There are three essentials to a great golf swing:

1. Keep your head still
2. Keep your stupid head still
3. Keep your goddamn stupid head still

If you managed to keep your head steady, it's probably because you locked your knees, lifted your shoulder, loosened your grip, and let your elbow fly

All of the basic movements of a perfectly executed golf swing can be easily duplicated by using a forceful turning motion of your body to toss a bag full of clubs into a pond

Few golfers are born with a natural talent for hitting the ball, but every player is blessed with the God-given ability to roll the ball over, kick it, knock it back in bounds, or throw it into the middle of the fairway

A golf match is a test of your skill against your opponent's sheer dumb luck

A fool and his money make excellent golfing companions

Good sportsmanship is as essential to the game of golf as good penmanship is to stock car racing

The lower the stakes in any match,
the more outrageous the behavior of
the competitors

There is no such thing as a friendly wager

Golfers who claim they never cheat
also lie

Never leave your opponent with
the sole responsibility for thinking of
all the things that might go wrong with
his shot

Counting on your opponent to
inform you when he breaks a rule
is like expecting him to make fun of
his own haircut

If your opponent hasn't played the
course before, don't be a spoilsport
and ruin all the surprises

Good golf manners require you to help
a competitor search for a lost ball, but
nothing says you have to find it

If you're the only one who improves your
lie, it's cheating; if you all improve your
lies, it's a reasonable allowance for unfair
playing conditions

Don't needle your partner

Don't talk in your own backswing

Always limp with the same leg for
the whole round

The score a player reports on
any hole should always be regarded
as his opening offer

Never subtract so many strokes on
any one hole that you wind up with
the honor on the next tee

The statute of limitations on forgotten
strokes is one hole

In any best-ball match, the smaller the significance of your partner's putt, the greater the probability that he will sink it

Taking more than two strokes to get down on a lightning-fast, steeply sloped green is no embarrassment unless you had to hit a wedge between the putts

It's surprisingly easy to hole a 50-foot putt when you lie 10

Whenever there is money riding
on a hole, someone will appear riding on
a mower

The putt for all the marbles will be on
a green they just sprayed with something
that makes you dizzy

Never play anyone for money who carries a 1-iron, has a tattoo, doesn't wear a glove, and can bounce a ball off the face of a sand wedge more than ten times in a row

Never play with anyone who would question an 8

Never take a check from anyone who uses a bag tag as I.D.

You can hear a clap of thunder from a hundred miles away when you're three holes down with three to play

Murphy's
SHORT GAME FUNDAMENTALS

No putt ever got shorter as a result
of being marked

A chip shot will always travel
one-third of the distance to the hole,
or twelve-thirds of the distance

A practice shot hit from a bunker after
a flubbed sand wedge will always stop
right next to the hole

The key to mastering the short shots
is to make sure you don't start hitting
them until you get within 100 yards
of the green

A ball hit to the wrong green will land
two feet from the hole

A ball hit to your green will stop an inch
from where the hole was yesterday

The only time you can ever suck back
a ball is when it lands 30 feet short

If you take the pin out, the ball will rocket over the hole

If you leave the pin in, it will bang the ball off the green

If you tend the pin, it will jam in the cup

Putts come three to a package

The green often forgets which way
the last putt broke

Every putt is a straight putt if you hit
the damn thing hard enough

There are no lip-ins

Misread putts have perfect pace;
on-line putts never reach the hole

Spike marks never turn a putt
towards the cup

Never lag a tap-in

Never putt a gimme

It's not a gimme if you're still away

You can't teach touch

You can't learn luck

The yips are contagious, but no one
catches a pure putting stroke

The grain of the green always runs towards the setting sun, except when it doesn't

After the first putt sinks, the hole shrinks

The trouble with the putting grip
is that one hand is not enough and
two hands are way too many

You can three-putt without plumb-bobbing
the break, but why take the chance?

Nonchalant putts
count the same as chalant putts

Even if it's longer than the fourth
one was, the fifth putt is always good

Always concede a putt if the ball cannot
be marked without the coin falling into
the cup

Murphy's
DICTATES OF GOLF ETIQUETTE

If you can't outrun a golf club, don't give advice

No one blows his nose at the end
of your follow-through

No one has a coughing fit as you walk
off the tee

No one rattles the ballwasher while
you're tying your shoes

No golfer ever played too fast

No group ever played too quietly

No golfer ever dressed too plainly

Never take lessons from your father

Never teach golf to your wife

Never play your son for money

Everyone replaces the divot
after a great shot

Everyone rakes the bunker after
a beautiful out

Everyone repairs the ball mark
after a fabulous putt

Everyone picks up the tab when they're
playing alone

Never steal a lost ball until it
stops rolling

Always replace divots in the fairway
and rake footprints in the sand traps
even if you have to move your ball
to do so

When another foursome is on the green ahead, "Fore!" is not an excuse, "So what?" is not an apology, and "Up yours" is not an explanation

Remember, it only takes a moment to pick up a wedge left on the green by a group of slow players in front of you and windmill it into a pond

No matter how early your tee time, there will always be a foursome in the middle of the first fairway

If you ever par the first three holes, you'll have a twenty-minute wait on the next tee

The only really useful golf tip is one given to the starter to get you out ahead of a mixed foursome

Slow players are early risers

Play is always faster on the other nine

The course marshal is a retired mortician
with cataracts and the shakes

If the course is completely empty when you drive up, it's because an outing of 100 golfers is about to tee off in a shotgun start or they're aerating the greens

If you aren't paired with the two loud-mouthed dickheads you saw unloading their clubs in the parking lot, it's because the couple from hell is waiting for you on the first tee

The greatest mystery in golf is how come players who can hit 100 balls on the range in ten minutes flat cannot make 94 strokes out on the course in anything under five hours

Even if she lies 22, never in the entire history of golf has a lady player ever picked up her ball